Famous Artists in History

FAMOUS ARTISTS
in History

15 PAINTERS, SCULPTORS, AND PHOTOGRAPHERS YOU SHOULD KNOW

—————— Kelly Milner Halls ——————

Illustrated by Amy Blackwell

ROCKRIDGE PRESS

Series Designer: Heather Krakora
Interior and Cover Designer: Lisa Forde
Art Producer: Alyssa Williams
Editor: Julie Haverkate
Production Editor: Holland Baker
Production Manager: Holly Haydash

Illustration © 2021 Amy Blackwell

Paperback ISBN: 978-1-63878-219-3 | eBook ISBN: 978-1-63878-860-7
R0

THIS BOOK IS DEDICATED TO
my artistic influences—
my father, Gene, who loved to paint,
and my daughter, Nessa,
who can do all things artistic.
I love you!

Contents

Introduction viii

Michelangelo BUONARROTI 1

Gian Lorenzo BERNINI 7

Utagawa HIROSHIGE 13

Julia Margaret CAMERON 19

Berthe MORISOT 25

Vincent VAN GOGH 31

Pablo PICASSO 37

Augusta SAVAGE 43

Frida KAHLO 49

Gordon PARKS 55

Andy WARHOL 61

Yayoi KUSAMA 67

Jaune Quick-to-See SMITH 73

Jean-Michel BASQUIAT 79

Njideka AKUNYILI CROSBY 85

Glossary **91**

References **95**

Introduction

Famous painter and sculptor Pablo Picasso once said, "Every child is an artist. The problem is how to remain an artist once we grow up."

Creators who protect and encourage that artistic spark born in childhood grow up to transform the world into a more beautiful and thoughtful place to live. Through their courageous efforts, artists offer everyone permission to see and feel things in their own special ways. In this way, artists celebrate individuality. This book examines 15 of those creative people who took their artistic passions to new heights as they grew up, grew famous, and even grew old.

The biographies of all 15 artists explore the stories of their lives. These are stories about growing up, stories about learning how to become an artist, and stories about following their passion for art. Several of the artists in this book struggled with mental illness. This is a difficult topic to discuss, but an important piece of their life stories. If you have any questions about this issue, please seek out a trusted adult to discuss them.

In the pages to come, you'll find out how Michelangelo Buonarroti became an expert in human anatomy, how

Frida Kahlo learned to paint, and the real meaning behind Vincent van Gogh's painting *Starry Night*. Each artist's biography includes a memorable quote, a fun fact, and a way to learn more. If you see a bolded word you don't quite understand, flip to the back of the book where you'll discover a glossary that defines that term.

Some of the artists may be familiar to you—such as Italian painter and sculptor Michelangelo or Dutch painter Vincent van Gogh. Others could be new to you—including Japanese master Utagawa Hiroshige who inspired European painters like Claude Monet. Nineteenth-century British photographer Julia Margaret Cameron, whose **portraits** captured the faces of her time, might also be new to you.

Familiar or not, all 15 are great artists. But calling them "the best" would be a mistake. Art is subjective. That means one person might love a painting, even if another person hates it. Beauty is in the eye of the beholder. No one can prove one artist is "the best." But we can study art and artists to find our personal favorites.

You'll explore different periods of artistic creation, like Michelangelo's Renaissance and Augusta Savage's **Harlem Renaissance**. You'll also learn about different art styles, like Hiroshige's woodblock prints, and read about how some artists helped create brand-new styles, like Pablo Picasso's contributions to Cubism.

Once you've explored these expert painters, sculptors, photographers, and multimedia artists, you'll have laid the groundwork for a lifelong path to creative discovery. If the world is very lucky, that path will help you create artwork of your own.

Don't be afraid to dive into art. You can't do it wrong. Your art can grow and change along with your body and your mind. Every step you take, and every painting or sculpture or photograph or collage you bring to life, is a lovely page in your artistic book of life.

Fame isn't the purpose of art. Self-expression is at the heart of every masterpiece. So, create to be seen and heard. Fame may follow one day, but even if it doesn't, your art will live on. It will find a place in the world, and so will you.

Michelangelo
BUONARROTI
1475—1564

Michelangelo Buonarroti was one of the most gifted sculptors and painters of all time. He lived during the Renaissance, a time when people moved away from living for God and the hope of going to heaven to celebrating life on Earth. Michelangelo wasn't sure what to believe, so his work reflected his love of God and the beauty of life.

Michelangelo was born in Caprese, a small town near Florence, Italy. His father was the town magistrate—a judge who settled legal disagreements. His mother was young and too ill to care for Michelangelo, so his first weeks were spent with a nurse and her stonecutter husband. His nurse went on to become his nanny.

After he moved the family to Florence, Michelangelo's father dreamed of starting a business his sons could run in the big city. But Michelangelo had grown up with a stonecutter in his life, and he wanted to be an artist. At 13, Michelangelo was **apprenticed** to a painter named Domenico Ghirlandaio. The painter lived in the household of Lorenzo de' Medici, a wealthy man who paid artists to create masterpieces.

De' Medici had one of the finest art collections in Europe. Michelangelo could walk freely among the collection, studying and improving his own work. As a young boy he carved the head of a satyr—a mythical man with the ears of a goat. De' Medici was impressed but teased him, saying such an old satyr wouldn't have perfect teeth. Michelangelo chiseled the teeth to address the criticism and won de' Medici's favor. His career was all but guaranteed.

After de' Medici died in 1492, Michelangelo was lost. He turned to the religious men of the Monastery of Santo Spirito for shelter. At 17, he began to study the human form by examining the bodies of patients who died in the monastery hospital. To thank the monks, Michelangelo carved a wooden statue of Jesus dying on the cross. This crucifix proved Michelangelo's knowledge of the human body included lifelike muscle details. It was his first true masterpiece.

Five years later, Cardinal Jean Bilhères de Lagraulas paid Michelangelo to create a marble sculpture for a chapel in the Old St. Peter's Basilica. Chip by chip, he created the *Pietà*. The statue features Mary, the mother of Jesus, with her son's lifeless body draped across her knees. Every detail masterfully carved in stone, from Mary's expression of grief to the limp arms and legs of Jesus, proved Michelangelo was extraordinary.

"THE TRUE WORK OF ART IS BUT A SHADOW OF THE DIVINE PERFECTION."

By 1501, the 25-year-old Michelangelo had taken on a new challenge. After sculptors damaged a huge, 13-foot piece of marble, Michelangelo claimed it, determined to release the artwork hidden within the stone. In 1504, Michelangelo unveiled *David*, a tribute to the Jewish king who killed Goliath in Biblical stories. He stands naked, in a peaceful pose, and the anatomy is perfect. Every limb and muscle looks as if it could spring into movement.

Michelangelo apprenticed with a painter. He knew how to paint, but he considered himself a sculptor. In 1508, Pope Julius II asked Michelangelo to paint the ceiling of the Sistine Chapel in Rome. At first he refused, suggesting there were better painters to tackle the challenge. But he finally took the job and crafted one of the finest works of art in human history.

In 33 individual paintings called panels, Michelangelo illustrated Genesis, the first book of the Bible. Each panel captures some part of God's creation of life on Earth. In the famous panel *Creation of Adam*, God's outstretched finger very nearly touches the finger of Adam, the first man named in the Bible.

Michelangelo invested four years in the ceiling of the Sistine Chapel. Pope Julius was so impatient with the painter's delays, he once struck him with a staff. Offended, Michelangelo refused to continue until the pope apologized.

Michelangelo was determined never to paint again, but he gave in when the pope asked him to paint a mural on the wall of the Sistine Chapel. He painted *The Last Judgment*. The mural reveals Jesus passing judgment on the sins of mankind. Biblical characters, including Adam's wife, Eve, are shown being tortured by demons for their bad choices. Michelangelo finished the painting seven years later in 1541.

Michelangelo studied nature and the human body expertly and reproduced those facts accurately in his art. His legacy is recognition as a master of the Renaissance. That attention to detail defined the Renaissance. It redirected art to find a balance between religious ideals and scientific facts.

Even today, people visit Italy to admire Michelangelo's masterpieces. Modern artists like Simone Kocher sometimes adapt Michelangelo's paintings to reflect new ideas. Kocher so admired Michelangelo's *Creation of Adam*, she painted *Creation of Eva* in 2018.

Collectors display photographs or miniature replicas of Michelangelo's work in their homes around the world. Posters, T-shirts, journals, shower curtains, and even a Teenage Mutant Ninja Turtle reflect the reach of the artistic master. And though Michelangelo died in 1564, just a month before his 89th birthday, his name lives on as synonymous with great artistry.

EXPLORE MORE! Michelangelo sculpted marble, but you could use soap and ice-pop sticks. What will your bar of soap become? The answer is in your imagination.

DID YOU KNOW? In 1503, Michelangelo and Leonardo da Vinci competed in a paint-off, but circumstances ended the competition almost immediately and neither artist won.

Gian Lorenzo
BERNINI
1598–1680

Gian Lorenzo Bernini was an Italian artist and the creator of Baroque art. Baroque captured the emotion, drama, physical energy, and perfect anatomy of artistic subjects. Bernini told stories in stone, carving movement and facial expressions in massive slabs of marble. He designed chapels, gardens, fountains, and other structures. He also painted portraits for wealthy customers called patrons.

Bernini was born in Naples, Italy, in 1598, and his father moved the family to Rome eight years later. As a boy, Bernini watched his father work as a sculptor, creating artistic statues for leaders of the Catholic Church and repairing damaged statues for wealthy patrons. Once he started training in his father's studio, it was clear he was a child prodigy, a young artist born with a special gift.

At 13, Bernini revealed his growing skill set when he presented a bust, a sculpture of the shoulders and head, of a doctor named Antonio Coppola. He claimed he'd done similar busts as an eight-year-old. Most people doubted the claim, but they could not deny Bernini's natural talent.

Paying jobs soon followed. By the time Bernini entered his 20s, Cardinal Scipione Borghese hired him to create four stone monuments for his large Roman estate. In just seven years, Bernini sculpted eight fictional Roman characters.

Even early in his career, Bernini's Baroque style was emerging. He mastered fine detail in marble, including the precise look of skin, fabric, fur, and plant life. By 1621, he was knighted by the pope and named a leader of the artists' academy in Rome. Bernini seemed to live a charmed life.

Like Michelangelo, one of Bernini's most famous marble sculptures was a likeness of the Jewish King David about to battle with Goliath. Michelangelo sculpted a calm, naked David standing upright before battle. But Bernini sculpted the moment that David prepared to launch the stone that killed the giant. He was active, with a determined look on his face. That emotional change defined Baroque art and won praise from Rome's artistic world and from the cardinal.

The sculpture Bernini created for Cardinal Borghese of Apollo trying to kidnap Daphne is also considered one of his greatest works. In this moment from Greek mythology, Apollo fell in love with Daphne, but she refused to marry him. She asked her father, the river god Peneus, to allow her to change form and escape Apollo.

Bernini's statue captures the shock on Apollo's face and the moment Daphne's fingers transform into branches right before his eyes. Apollo's emotional facial expressions, Daphne's windblown hair, her branch-like hands, and the fabric rippling in motion all make this sculpture a masterpiece.

Bernini was also hired to create the Baldacchino—a bronze canopy meant to add to the beauty of St. Peter's tomb. The 94-foot-tall structure has four columns that seem to twist as they reach for the heavens. Sculpted bees are scattered throughout the structure. Bernini also created four 14-foot-tall figures, thoughtfully placed within the canopy. He continued to remodel the historic Basilica for decades, proving his skill as a sculptor and an architect. His understanding and use of natural light to spotlight the work set him apart from other Italian sculptors.

In the 1640s, Cardinal Federico Cornaro asked Bernini to create a sculpture to decorate what would become his burial place in Rome's Santa Maria della Vittoria church.

This became Bernini's most emotional work, *The Ecstasy of Saint Teresa*. Saint Teresa supposedly slipped into a dream state when she talked to God. Bernini's sculpture captures a fainting Saint Teresa with an angel floating by her side. Smaller statues of Cornaro and other Catholic leaders are to the left and right of the powerful scene, as if they are witnesses to the saint's prayerful moments.

The Ecstasy of Saint Teresa is considered one of the most perfect examples of Baroque art for its mastery of capturing human drama and emotion and perfect anatomical detail.

When Bernini was called to France in 1665 by King Louis XIV, he was asked to create a sculpture of the king on his horse. Louis XIV was displeased with the final project, and had his royal masons alter Bernini's work. But the bust Bernini sculpted of the king, complete with armor and delicate lace, is considered one of his finest works.

Bernini was not content to copy sculptors like Michelangelo who had come before him. He wanted to add fire and emotional content to works of art. He wanted his art to resemble true life and remind admirers of every human sensation.

Before Bernini's Baroque movement, art was meant to touch the mind; after Bernini, art was meant to touch the mind and the soul. Artists focused on the physical before Bernini led them to capture human emotion along with physicality. Every flicker of emotion that crosses the subject's face and every muscle that contracts during movement is captured in Baroque. Defined by Bernini, Baroque architecture made a lasting impact on the city of Rome.

Adding such passion to his work drew some criticism. New practices are often criticized. But time proved Bernini's Baroque movement could survive and earn love from art fans worldwide.

EXPLORE MORE! Can't make it to New York? Search for "Gian Lorenzo Bernini" on MetMuseum.org to explore a variety of the artist's works.

DID YOU KNOW? When Bernini was 20, he started painting self-portraits—a LOT of them. He probably painted more self-portraits than any other 17th-century artist.

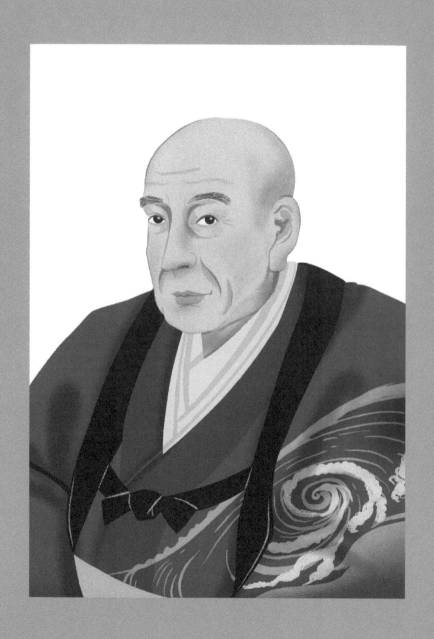

Utagawa HIROSHIGE

1797—1858

U tagawa Hiroshige was one of the masters of the ancient Japanese ukiyo-e woodblock printing tradition, which made art affordable for all people. Before woodblock prints, art in Japan had been reserved for the wealthy. By carving images into wooden blocks and applying layers of ink, color by color, Hiroshige created graceful pictures.

Little has been recorded about Hiroshige's youth. He lost both his parents by the age of 12. It's unknown what sparked Hiroshige's interest in art, or why he chose printmaking specifically. But before Hiroshige's father died, he passed his job as a fire warden on to Hiroshige. The paycheck made it possible for Hiroshige to study art and pay the bills.

Hiroshige's teacher, Utagawa Toyohiro, taught him to create ukiyo-e block prints. Using carved wooden images of warriors called **samurai**, actors, or beautiful women, Hiroshige made copies of portraits on paper called *Kizuki Hosho*. He created prints one layer at a time: first, the outline in black; next, the clothing and lips in red; then the hair in black. He added his signature last, in Japanese lettering called kanji.

By the time he turned 21 in 1818, Hiroshige saw his first artwork published. He married Okabe Yuaemon in 1821 and had a son, Nakajiro, the same year.

After his teacher died in 1828, Hiroshige moved from portraits to landscapes. Unlike other artists, Hiroshige added animals and people to the landscapes. In 1832, Hiroshige passed his fire warden job on to his son, and pursued art full-time.

For decades, Hiroshige perfected his woodblock landscapes. He journeyed on foot from Edo to Kyoto on the Tokaido road—a trip that took 10 to 16 days—and observed the joy and excitement of travel. His *Fifty-Three Stations of the Tokaido* series reflects that energy and became one of his most popular sets of images. Because it shows people living ordinary lives along the road, it was unique and engaging.

Station of Otsu from the *Fifty-Three Stations* series reflects Japan's love of travel. Instead of capturing the simple geography of the coast, Hiroshige explored a busy city street, alive with human activity and color. Common ukiyo-e at the time captured simple landscapes with **muted** colors and no action in the image. People didn't normally appear in block prints before Hiroshige, and certainly not lively people. Combining Japanese people with the beauty of nature distinguished Hiroshige's art. He made humanity part of the landscape in a new way.

> **"I LEAVE MY BRUSH IN THE EAST, AND SET FORTH ON MY JOURNEY. I SHALL SEE THE FAMOUS PLACES IN THE WESTERN LAND."**

Naruto Whirlpool, Awa Province captures the power of nature and its impact on humanity. Blue waves capped with white foam crash over charcoal-gray rocks as people look on. Whirlpools break up the waves and add more tension to the artwork.

Hiroshige's *Kinryuzan Temple at Asakusa* reveals another new approach to the woodblock print. In this print, he dressed the ancient **Buddhist** temple in snow, with a fiery red gate and a red building in the distance. People with umbrellas walk along a snowy path, beneath a giant red lantern. The high contrast in colors of the white snow and the red objects was innovative in woodblock printing.

When the great Tenpo famine made food scarce from 1833 to 1837, Hiroshige's wife sold her belongings to support her husband's artwork. She died in 1839, and Hiroshige grieved. But eventually, he worked as an artist again. Because he was paid very little for each print, he had to create and sell thousands of prints to survive. This affordable art made it possible for ordinary people to decorate their homes. Before woodblock prints like Hiroshige's, only the rich could buy art.

In time, Hiroshige became an art teacher. As he grew older, he became a Buddhist monk—a holy man. He continued to make art as a monk, including his last series of prints called *One Hundred Famous Views of Edo*.

He died in the Japanese **cholera epidemic** of 1858. During his lifetime, Hiroshige produced between 5,000 and 8,000 individual woodblock prints. Many survive in museums and homes around the world. Modern scanning and printing technology allow today's art lovers to display his work in their homes as well.

Hiroshige was one of the last masters of ukiyo-e artwork. He was heavily influenced by both Japanese and European art traditions. And in return, he influenced artists of the European tradition like Claude Monet, Vincent van Gogh, James Whistler, Paul Gauguin, and Frank Lloyd Wright, all of whom discovered his artwork after his death and loved it. Vincent van Gogh made copies of Hiroshige's prints to teach himself new techniques. Some say Van Gogh's use of bright color was partially influenced by Hiroshige. Other artists admired his use of trees and flowers to enrich his landscapes.

The influence of Japanese artists like Hiroshige on Western painters is called Japonism. Whistler's painting *Caprice in Purple and Gold* features a woman gazing at one of Hiroshige's prints. Global citizens who owned Hiroshige's artwork were considered sophisticated, whether they owned landscapes or his early portraits.

Even modern pop artist Julian Opie and painter Nigel Caple have studied Hiroshige's approach to landscapes to create their own masterpieces. Hiroshige's influence lives on.

EXPLORE MORE! Would your drawing take on more personality if you added animals and people? Let's find out! Draw a picture of a mountain and its valley without living things. Then draw a copy of that picture with people and animals added. Which one do you like best?

DID YOU KNOW? Ukiyo-e means "pictures of the floating world." It refers to woodblock prints capturing the floating world, or entertainment, of the time, such as warriors, actors, dancers, and wrestlers.

Julia Margaret
CAMERON
1815 — 1879

After Julia Margaret Cameron married her husband, Charles, gave birth to five children, raised five more children, adopted another daughter, and ushered all those children into lives of their own, the 48-year-old woman embarked on a remarkable career taking photographic portraits and advancing the science of a brand-new art form.

Born in Calcutta, India, on June 11, 1815, British citizen Julia Margaret Pattle was the second of seven sisters in her family. Her father worked as an executive at the East India Company. Her mother came from a wealthy French family.

Cameron was unusual for a girl born in the early 19th century. She was dramatic and lively at a time when girls were supposed to be quiet and ladylike. People sometimes called her **eccentric**, but she didn't care. She studied in France and traveled the world with her family, exploring France, India, South Africa, and Great Britain.

On her travels, Cameron met important people, including the man she would marry, Charles Hay Cameron, in 1838, when she was 23. Famed British astronomer Sir John Herschel introduced her to photography four years later, but she wouldn't take up the occupation for another 20 years. Cameron became a member of high society, hosting writers, artists, politicians, and scientists at her home.

When she was 48, one of her daughters gave her a camera hoping it would entertain her. Cameron fell in love with the art form and captured special portraits of her friends and household staff. Those portraits made Julia Margaret Cameron famous.

One of Cameron's friends, the famous poet Alfred, Lord Tennyson, introduced her to the eight-year-old daughter of a family he knew. In 1864, Cameron found great happiness creating a portrait of the girl, Annie Wilhelmina Philpot.

Cameron called the portrait *Annie, My First Success*. She felt the picture of a child dressed in a lovely dark **Victorian-era** coat with her hair hanging loose down her shoulders captured the look of innocence. Since children during that time were considered tiny adults, the photo seemed ideal.

When Cameron saw the image, she was delighted. She ran through her home, searching for a gift for Annie as a thank-you for posing for the portrait.

That same year, Cameron staged a photo she found personally important. Called *Madonna and Child*,

> **"I LONGED TO ARREST ALL BEAUTY THAT CAME BEFORE ME, AND AT LENGTH THE LONGING HAS BEEN SATISFIED."**

it is meant to remind the viewer of the Virgin Mary (Madonna) and Jesus (the child). Experts said the photograph proved Cameron was well-read in history and religion. They called the photograph "high art," meaning it was serious and important. At the time, cameras were a new technology. Photographs were considered playful, but not artistic. "High art" meant Julia Cameron had uplifted photography.

Two years later, in 1866, Cameron gathered her children, including her adopted daughter, Mary Ryan, and took *May Day*. Ryan looked so beautiful in the picture, a man named Sir Henry Cotton fell in love with the young woman and asked her to marry him. She agreed. Cameron later provided photographs to illustrate two volumes of Tennyson's poetry.

In 1867, Cameron convinced her old friend John Herschel to pose for a portrait. Herschel introduced Cameron to the science of photography when she was a newlywed, and their warm relationship had grown strong over the years.

In the photograph, Herschel wears a cape and a dark velvet hat and gazes into the distance. Wild strands of his silver hair escape the hat, making him look energetic.

Cameron thought the bags under Herschel's eyes made him appear determined in his scientific studies. In fact, that was Cameron's aim. She wanted to document Herschel, but she also wanted to celebrate the power of "great men of science."

Dramatically posed, gently blurred portraits became Cameron's signature practice. It made her subjects look mysterious and set her apart from other photographers.

When naturalist **Charles Darwin** and his family rented a cottage nearby in 1868, Cameron was determined to take his portrait. He wasn't sure at first, but finally gave in. Not only did she capture a striking photo of Darwin, but also she helped support her family. She pioneered a more commercial element of portraiture by selling lots of copies for money. Cameron sold copies of the Darwin portrait in London. Autographed copies went for more money.

Though Cameron blurred her first images by accident, she refined the effect to add an artistic quality to her photographs. That choice helped elevate photography into the world of fine art. She hoped to capture the spiritual quality of her subjects and the blur helped her succeed.

The fact that she was a woman held Cameron back in most artistic circles. Her male peers said she could not be a master photographer because she was a woman. Cameron was unfazed. She said she had no desire to "master" anything. She simply wanted to create important art.

Cameron became well known for her pictures of children, which amazed those male peers. She confessed she had a secret weapon—patience and trust. Without trust, she explained, good pictures of children were impossible. Photographers who learned that lesson from Cameron improved their portraits of children, too.

EXPLORE MORE! *Julia Margaret Cameron: The Complete Photographs* by Julian Cox, Colin Ford, Joanne Lukitsh, and Philippa Wright shows her full catalog of photographs and can be read online here: Getty.edu /publications/virtuallibrary/0892366818.html.

DID YOU KNOW? Cameron used negatives—glass coated with chemicals—to capture her images. Her subjects had to sit completely still for three to seven minutes for the photography to properly work.

Berthe
MORISOT
1841—1895

Berthe Morisot was a master of Impressionism, art that captures the feeling of a moment and not the exact look of it. Impressionist painters Claude Monet and Pierre-Auguste Renoir considered her one of the best. French art critics didn't take her seriously because she was a woman. The art critics were wrong. Morisot had serious talent.

Morisot was born to an upper-middle-class family in France in 1841. Her father was a civil servant, and her mother was the great-niece of the painter Jean-Honoré Fragonard. In a way, Morisot and her older sister Edma were born into the art world.

Both sisters wanted to paint professionally, but women were not allowed to attend art school. Private tutors taught them about famous painters—masters with paintings hanging at the Louvre, a museum in Paris. A very good painter, a man named Jean-Baptiste-Camille Corot, soon stepped in to continue their education.

Corot saw more promise in Edma's work, but Edma gave up her studies to marry and move away. In letters, Edma encouraged her sister to carry on, and she did. By 1864, Morisot had her first exhibit at the Salon de Paris, a yearly celebration of fine French art. It was a great honor, but the way men discouraged her made Morisot so insecure she destroyed many of her earliest paintings.

The tide began to turn when Morisot met painter Édouard Manet in 1868. He greatly admired her work and helped her become the only woman who was an official member of the Impressionists, a group of rising stars in the world of French painting.

In 1872, Morisot painted one of her most famous pieces, called *The Cradle*. It featured her sister Edma with her infant daughter, Blanche. Morisot was known for her likenesses of balconies and other small outdoor spaces. But this quiet, personal look at motherhood and affection indoors was a masterpiece. The contrast of Edma's pale skin against the room's dark drapes impressed art critics. And the flowing, nearly transparent look of the cloth over the baby's bed seemed almost magical in its gentleness.

Another of Morisot's most famous paintings is *Woman at Her Toilette*, from 1875. Male artists like Edgar Degas and Renoir were allowed to paint naked women figures in their dressing rooms. But it was considered improper for women to do so. Morisot did not give up. She painted a woman dressed in her undergarments, gazing into a mirror. Critics found it both classical and elegant with its soft shades of lavender, pink, blue, and white. It appealed to many people because it was beautiful, but not **risqué**.

In *Summer's Day*, Morisot celebrated a redesigned French park in 1879. Her two models were probably friends, seated in a rowboat, dressed in crisp hats and dresses, one with an umbrella in her lap. The painter's signature zigzag brushstrokes and her use of vibrant colors capture the magic of a warm summer day perfectly.

One of Morisot's rare paintings without a human figure is called *Le Jardin a Bougival* (*The Garden at Bougival* in English). It is a breathtaking portrait of flowers and greenery painted in 1884. Morisot spent summers near the garden between 1881 and 1884 and painted 40 works there. Her affection for the setting is clear in the colorful roses and softly painted leaves and grasses. Though her brushstrokes look almost random in dabs and dots, they bring the magic of the garden into beautiful focus.

One art critic said Morisot must have ground up flower petals and added them to her paint to capture such beauty.

Such praise was groundbreaking for the painter. She had earned her place among the Impressionist masters.

On the Terrace was painted in 1874 and went on exhibit in 1877. In it, Morisot painted a woman sitting on a terrace that overlooks a French seaside resort called Fécamp. Morisot was staying at the resort with her aunt, surrounded by the wealthy citizens of Paris. This painting features her typical fluttering brushstrokes, but it is distinctive because her subject, a beautifully dressed woman, is sitting off-center, far to the right within the painting. It is as if she's trapped in the space. Some say it was Morisot's way of expressing her forced limits as a painter and a woman.

Berthe Morisot's legacy is, in some ways, obvious. She proved that a woman could compete with men. Today, that may not seem like such a big deal. But in the early 19th century, women were controlled and confined by society's expectations that limited their behavior. Women had to stay home performing domestic duties like raising children and doing housework.

Morisot blurred the barriers previously set for women artists. In a world that fought to hold women back, Morisot's male friends lifted her up. She was a revolutionary, and her paintings are still admired today. She captured women with grace and respect, dark colors, and light. Her paintings were like beautiful dreams all people could admire. Her work and her determination proved to be her artistic legacy.

After Morisot died, her daughter, Julie, dedicated her life to making her mother's work more famous. Inspired by her mother, Julie was a painter, too.

EXPLORE MORE! The National Museum of Women in the Arts in Washington, DC, features some of Berthe Morisot's Impressionist paintings. You can study her brushstrokes there.

DID YOU KNOW? Morisot had many male painters as friends, but she rarely painted men. She focused instead on painting women the way she saw them.

Vincent
VAN GOGH
1853—1890

Thanks to paintings like *Starry Night* and *Irises,*
Vincent van Gogh is one of the most famous painters of the 19th century. His distinctive approach to color
and his personal style set his work apart from other artists of his time. He created more than 2,000 works of art
but died without knowing his work would be renowned
and celebrated.

Vincent van Gogh was born on March 30, 1853, in the
Netherlands, but very little is known about his early life.
His mother's name was Anna and his father, Theodorus
van Gogh, was a church pastor. Van Gogh had two
brothers—Theo and Cor—and three sisters—Elisabeth,
Anna, and Willemien.

Van Gogh was a quiet child who was emotional and
very insecure. He didn't display an interest in art in his
early life. He attended school, then worked at an important art gallery in The Hague, a city in the Netherlands.
At 16, he was their youngest clerk. In time, he was sent to

Paris and London as an art dealer, but he lost interest in buying and selling art.

Van Gogh wanted to do something more important, so he tried to become a minister. His parents sent him to **seminary** school, but he abandoned class to preach to a mining community in Belgium. He was fired for being too passionate.

He fell in love multiple times, and multiple times had his heart broken. His brother Theo encouraged him to become an artist. Van Gogh doubted his potential. His parents doubted, too. But Theo promised to support him while he learned to paint. Van Gogh's doubt never faded, but his talent took root.

Van Gogh's career lasted only 10 short years. In that time, he filled at least four paper sketchbooks, created 2,100 works of art, and learned how to see and draw common people and places. Experts agree he had no talent when he started. But his skills grew with every artistic step he took.

In 1885, as Van Gogh struggled to improve, he made *The Potato Eaters*, a black-and-white lithograph. It is one of only nine he ever created. A lithograph is a drawing carved in stone or metal so paper copies can be made with ink, like woodblock prints. Van Gogh used chalk to carve his lithograph original and questioned the choice of chalk in a letter to Theo. Once again, Van Gogh doubted himself.

Art critics hated the drawing of four poor people sitting around a table eating potatoes. It was

Post-impressionist in design, and more concerned with **symbolism** than accuracy. It lacked the bright colors used by French painters like Paul Gauguin. Critics said the faces, hands, and even the potatoes were ugly. Today, it is considered a masterpiece because it captures the deep sadness of a poor family so perfectly. But Van Gogh called it a failure.

Café Terrace at Night started as a rough drawing in a sketchbook, and Van Gogh painted the sketch in 1888. To capture the energy of the café—the light, the action, the people—Van Gogh set up his easel outside near the patio. He painted the furniture, the excitement he saw, and the joy it made him feel. The painting wasn't exactly what Van Gogh saw, but it captured his happiness and the Post-impressionist style of his day. It is one of his most popular paintings. The café was in Arles, France, and still exists there as the Café Van Gogh.

In 1889, *Starry Night* came to life. Painted in the Saint-Rémy mental **asylum**, it reflected how sad and lost Van Gogh felt. For most of his life he struggled with mental health challenges. This stay at Saint-Rémy was his last attempt to find peace.

Unlike most patients, Van Gogh had a great deal of freedom at the hospital. He could wander the gardens and was given a room to use as an art studio. As he considered taking his own life, he painted the swirls of the night sky to reflect his emotional storms. The dark colors mirrored his failing moods.

Today, people see the swirls as a celebration of the wind and the moonlight. They see the colors as the rich memories of a beautiful night sky. Art—especially the work of Van Gogh—inspires different feelings in different people.

On July 27, 1890, Vincent van Gogh succcumbed to his mental health challenges and died, with Theo, his brother and best friend, by his bedside. Van Gogh died believing he was a failure, having sold only one painting out of hundreds he had created.

The troubled artist never imagined he'd leave behind a rich, respected legacy in those paintings. Generations were influenced and inspired by Van Gogh's artwork. Millions have admired the brushstrokes of his original paintings in museums worldwide.

In fact, a popular new way to experience Van Gogh's works is through interactive tours at cities located around the world. These digital, **immersive** shows project Van Gogh's paintings inside huge rooms. You feel as though you're walking inside one of his paintings, through a field of irises or under the swirling night sky.

EXPLORE MORE! Explore Van Gogh's work from home by taking a virtual tour of the Van Gogh Museum in Amsterdam: VanGoghMuseum.nl/en.

DID YOU KNOW? Van Gogh produced a huge body of work during his short lifetime: 1,000 drawings, 150 watercolors, 9 lithographs, and 900 paintings.

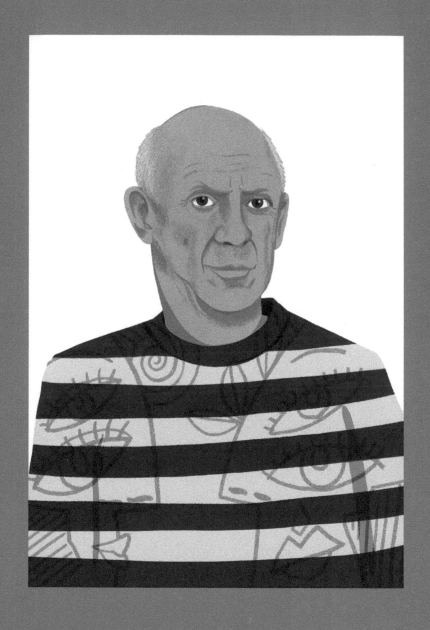

Pablo
PICASSO
1881—1973

Pablo Picasso was born to be an artistic genius. During his lifetime, Picasso produced more than 26,000 works of art and gained fame as a truly unusual painter. After he learned the classic elements of fine art, Picasso created new art forms of his own. He was a pioneer and a master.

Picasso was born in Spain and known by the name Pablo Ruiz Picasso—a combination of his first name, a name drawn from his father (Ruiz), and a name drawn from his mother (Picasso). Picasso's father was an art teacher and professional painter. The boy seemed destined to follow in his father's footsteps. Almost immediately, Picasso showed a skill for drawing. He was so obsessed with art, his other studies suffered. When he was sent to an empty room as punishment, he was delighted. A sketchbook was all he needed.

By the time he was 13, Picasso had been accepted into the school where his father taught in La Coruña, Spain. That same year, he had mastered neoclassical oil painting—formal painting inspired by ancient Roman techniques.

When Picasso's seven-year-old sister Conchita grew ill with **diphtheria**, Picasso promised God he would stop painting if she survived. When she died, art was his only comfort. At 16, his father sent him to the Royal Academy of San Fernando in Madrid, but he promptly quit the classes and set out on his own. Picasso wanted to create art in a distinctive way.

Picasso started *The Old Guitarist* in 1903. It is a work known as one of his finest creations because the colors and the odd angles added so much to the story. It features a **frail**, old guitarist painted in light and dark tones of blue oil paint. It was created during Picasso's Blue Period, a time when he used rich tones of blue in his artwork. The old man is slumped, cross-legged over a brown guitar. He seems sad, exhausted, and his bare shoulder protrudes from a rip in his tattered shirt.

After his Blue Period, Picasso slid into his Rose Period. By the end of the period, in 1905, Picasso painted a portrait of writer Gertrude Stein. The author and the artist became friends when Picasso moved to France.

Stein was influential in the worlds of art and literature. Her approval advanced Picasso's status as a master. Painting the portrait was his way of thanking Stein for her support. It is a traditional painting showing Stein seated and leaning forward with a gruff look on her face. Her dark hair is pulled back, and her dark coat nearly

"THE WORLD TODAY DOESN'T MAKE SENSE, SO WHY SHOULD I PAINT PICTURES THAT DO?"

matches her hair. Her pale hands are resting in front of her, near her knees.

Stein's face seems to glow against the darkness. Experts say this is because Picasso was not happy with her original expression and repainted it after the rest of the portrait was complete. Stein donated the painting to the Metropolitan Museum of Art in New York in 1946.

Picasso soon began creating artwork known as Cubism. In Cubism, the way things realistically looked were reduced to the geometric shape of cubes. Traditionally rounded shapes like heads and fruits were squared off without explanation.

When Picasso explored surrealism—a movement that explored dreamlike visions—he took a more circular approach. This can be seen in his painting *Girl Before a Mirror*, finished in 1932. The brightly colored girl looking at her reflection looks happy. But her shadowed reflection seems to be crying. Picasso was simultaneously exploring what we see when we look in a mirror—the outer image—and what we're feeling inside. His use of vibrant colors and distorted shapes made this painting special and it was also one of his favorites.

Later in his career, Picasso's sharp lines and use of bright colors transformed his paintings, including *The Weeping Woman*, painted in 1937. It features one of his many romantic partners, Dora Maar. The painting was Picasso's reaction to the destruction and emotional pain inflicted by the Spanish Civil War. Picasso painted several weeping women portraits, but this bright, almost shocking, work in red, green, white, yellow, and blue is considered one of his finest.

Picasso was an artist who dipped his brush into many styles and mediums. He painted traditional oil portraits of people he admired in Spain. He also painted surrealistic works that defied those traditions. He made lithographs that poorer art lovers could afford. He even created ceramic plates, **medallions**, and sculptures. All his work is admired and exhibited around the world.

Painters like Britain's David Hockney were inspired to break artistic rules by studying Picasso's body of work, which changed as Picasso did. Museums proudly exhibit every form of Picasso's artistic style, proof of his enduring popularity.

The women he loved during his life often inspired Picasso's work. The people who love his creations are eternally grateful.

EXPLORE MORE! Picasso is best known for his Cubist work. To learn more about Cubism, look up Juan Gris and Georges Braque. See which Cubist you might most admire.

DID YOU KNOW? In 2018, a crowd of 25,000 people paid $50 each to buy a portion of *Musketeer Bust*, a portrait of a man created by Picasso in 1968. Where it will hang is uncertain.

Augusta
SAVAGE
1892—1962

Augusta Savage was an African American sculptor who helped usher in an art period known as the Harlem Renaissance. She had a passion for art and fought for her creative place in the world and found success.

Augusta Savage was born in Green Cove Springs, Florida, on February 29, 1892. She was the seventh of 14 children of Methodist minister Edward Fells and his wife, Cornelia.

From an early age, Savage fell in love with sculpting animal figures using red clay she dug from the ground near her home. Her father did not approve. He treated her very badly, nearly causing her to give up on her artistic dreams.

Savage married John T. Moore in 1907 when she was barely 15. A year later, she gave birth to a daughter, Irene. Soon after, she was a **widow** living with her parents. When they moved to West Palm Beach in 1915, there was no clay for Savage to dig and sculpt.

Four years later, in 1919, a local artist gave her some clay. Savage sculpted a group of figures and entered them in the West Palm Beach County Fair. The figures won a special prize and Savage knew sculpting was her destiny.

Savage left her daughter with her parents to be sure Irene would be safe and fed. Then she moved to New York City. It was a difficult choice, but she made it with only $4.60 in her pocket.

Savage moved to New York City to be a part of the Harlem Renaissance—the birth of art by talented Black creators—and a member of the Black art community. She sculpted her nephew, Ellis Ford, in 1929 wearing a newsboy cap and a wrinkled shirt collar. She named the work *Gamin*, a slang term for a streetwise kid. The sculpture won Savage the Julius Rosenwald Fellowship. The fellowship money allowed her to study art in Europe. *Gamin* gained Augusta respect and a chance to teach other Black artists how to sculpt.

In 1932, Savage returned to Harlem and opened the Savage Studio of Arts and Crafts, where she taught young Black artists her trade. She was invited to make a sculpture for the 1939 New York World's Fair. Inspired by "Lift Every Voice and Sing," a song written by civil rights activist James Weldon Johnson, Savage created a 16-foot-tall harp, with 12 standing Black gospel singers representing its strings. The back of the harp, called a sounding board, was the hand and arm of God. A kneeling Black man holding sheet music was the harp's foot pedal.

> **"I HAVE CREATED NOTHING REALLY BEAUTIFUL, REALLY LASTING. BUT IF I CAN INSPIRE ONE OF THESE YOUNGSTERS ... MY MONUMENT WILL BE IN THEIR WORK."**

Considered the most photographed work on exhibit at the fair, Savage named the work after the song, but the fair retitled it *The Harp*. When the fair ended, Savage couldn't afford to move or store the masterpiece. *Lift Every Voice and Sing* was turned to rubble despite its incredible beauty.

That same year, Savage opened the Salon of Contemporary Negro Art in Harlem. *Diving Boy* was one of her sculptures exhibited there. Cast in bronze, it features a young Black boy about to dive into imaginary water.

Savage gave the celebrated sculpture to Ninah Cummer, the wife of wealthy Florida lumber magnate Arthur Cummer, in 1940. It stood at the end of the Cummers' reflecting pond for years, before it went on permanent display at the Cummer Museum in 1961.

In 1942, Savage went back to her roots, sculpting *Portrait of a Baby* in red **terra-cotta** clay. The lifelike face of an infant seems to be resting on an orange, stone pillow, or within the palm of a loving hand, as its eyes gaze upward.

Savage captured her vision of folk legend John Henry's young face in 1940. John Henry was a fictional strong man able to out-chisel a steam-powered rock drill with his sledgehammer. Her sculpture of a strong Black man helped the world see the beauty Savage saw.

Savage's sculpture featured a handsome man with piercing eyes, soft, full lips, and a confident expression. Like all her work, *Portrait Head of John Henry* celebrated the strength and beauty of Black Americans. That positive representation set Savage's work apart from that of other sculptors.

Augusta Savage has a brilliant legacy as a pillar of the Harlem Renaissance. The artwork she created, even when only photos of those pieces survived, established the importance of Black artists and represented the beauty and intelligence of Black Americans. She found the courage to sculpt that beauty less than 100 years after slavery had been outlawed. Her courage gave other Black women a beacon to follow to create distinctive art of their own. She encouraged other Black creators to prove their points of view were important, too.

Ultimately, Savage believed her richest legacy lived on in the many Black children she taught to create art of their own. That art, rooted in her incomparable skills and encouragement, was what she considered her proudest contribution.

EXPLORE MORE! To learn more about Augusta Savage, explore her work at the New-York Historical Society at NYHistory.org/exhibitions/augusta-savage -renaissance-woman.

DID YOU KNOW? Augusta Savage became the first Black woman in the National Association of Women Painters and Sculptors in 1934.

Frida
KAHLO
1907—1954

Frida Kahlo was a Mexican-born painter who created her own style of painting, inspired by symbolism, surrealism, and realism—the artistic style that tries to re-create exactly what the artist has seen. Her works, often self-portraits, are filled with vibrant colors and are sometimes joyful, sometimes heartbreaking.

Frida Kahlo was born in Mexico City, Mexico, in 1907. Her father, Carl Wilhelm Kahlo, was a German photographer who moved to Mexico and married Kahlo's mother, Matilda. Kahlo was one of four daughters.

Polio struck Kahlo when she was only six. For nine months she was bedridden. Her right leg and foot were impacted by the disease, causing her to limp when she recovered. When kids teased her at school, Kahlo started wearing long skirts to mask her disability.

Kahlo continued to play soccer, wrestle, and swim with her father. They were very close. He encouraged her to push past life's challenges, and she did.

When she was 15, Kahlo enrolled in the elite National Preparatory School in Mexico City. She was soon known for her passion for life and bravery in the face of any challenge.

Muralist Diego Rivera was hired by the school to paint his mural *The Creation*. Kahlo told her friends she would marry him someday. Before that happened, she was severely hurt in a bus accident.

For three months, Kahlo was in a body cast in bed. Her parents made a special easel so she could paint as she recovered. Kahlo soon found it would be her life's work.

A year later, Kahlo painted her first of many self-portraits. When she reconnected with Rivera in 1928, she asked him to critique her paintings. He encouraged her work and married her a year later. They both expressed their emotions and political beliefs through their paintings.

Kahlo traveled with her husband all over the United States, wherever he painted murals. She admired his murals, so when he told her to include more Mexican folk art in her work, she listened. Soon her self-portraits began to evolve from realistic to surrealistic in style. In 1932, she painted *Henry Ford Hospital*.

In the colorful painting, Kahlo lies on a hospital bed as six objects float around her body, each one connected to her by thin red threads. All six objects reflect some aspect of her feelings of sadness and loss. Kahlo's works are unique—like painted diaries.

> **"I PAINT SELF-PORTRAITS BECAUSE I AM SO OFTEN ALONE, BECAUSE I AM THE PERSON I KNOW BEST."**

In 1936, Kahlo painted *My Grandparents, My Parents, and I*. At the time, dictator Adolf Hitler was trying to take over all of Europe. Because he forbade interracial marriage, Kahlo protested through a painting. She painted portraits of her global ancestry. Kahlo painted herself as a small child in Mexico. Above her head, she painted her parents in their wedding clothes. And above her parents are her grandparents—one side German, the other side Spanish.

After her marriage to Diego Rivera ended in divorce in 1939, Kahlo painted *Self-Portrait with Cropped Hair*. Kahlo cut the long dark hair Rivera had loved. Some say it was a sign of grief. Others say it was a declaration of independence. In the painting, Kahlo is seated and dressed in a man's suit. Scissors in hand, Kahlo's long, black hair is scattered across a bloodred floor.

One of Kahlo's most famous self-portraits, also created in 1939, is *The Two Fridas*. Two painted versions of Kahlo sit side by side against a backdrop of gray, cloudy skies. On the left, Frida is dressed in a white gown of European design. Her heart is visible, torn, and bleeding. On the right, Frida is dressed in a traditional Mexican dress—her heart whole and healthy. Most agree it represents Kahlo's life before and after Diego Rivera.

Kahlo and Rivera remarried in 1940, but it was still a rocky relationship. In 1943, once again she expressed her despair in a self-portrait called *Thinking of Death*. After a lifetime of sickness, injury, and constant physical pain, Kahlo was keenly aware of how fragile the human body could be. She painted herself surrounded by green plants, a symbol of health. But a portal on her forehead reveals a skull and crossbones. Though she was thinking of death, she was also thinking of rebirth and being freed from a failing body.

Frida Kahlo didn't know her paintings were "surrealistic" until a friend told her they were. Her legacy is not tied to any artistic style. Her legacy is rooted in her courage. No matter how passionate her feelings might have been, she revealed them through her art in a distinctive way.

Kahlo finished around 200 paintings—55 of them self-portraits. She never shied away from telling her truth, even as the truth changed and evolved. She celebrated life and death, love and loss, a woman's power, and a woman's heartbreak.

Kahlo's work seems to say she would live on, no matter what fate delivered. By the time she died of pneumonia and pulmonary embolisms, or blood clots, on July 13, 1954, after 47 years of life, she had made her artistic mark on history. Frida Kahlo was one of Mexico's—and the world's—greatest painters because of who she was and the work she created.

EXPLORE MORE! To discover more about Frida Kahlo, read Susan B. Katz's *The Story of Frida Kahlo: A Biography Book for New Readers*. Or explore her work online at Frida-Kahlo-Foundation.org.

DID YOU KNOW? Kahlo proudly embraced traditional Mexican dress when the women around her were wearing European styles. As a fashion and cultural icon, she has been celebrated in Barbie's Inspiring Women Series, and on Halloween in 2014, pop star Beyoncé put her hair up, drew in eyebrows, and wore a floral headpiece and a colorful gown in honor of the artist. (That same Halloween, Beyoncé's husband, Jay Z, dressed as another famous artist: Jean-Michel Basquiat, who you can read more about on pages 79–83.)

Gordon
PARKS
1912—2006

Throughout the decades that Gordon Parks took pictures, he got to know the people he photographed. He learned what stories they had to tell, and he created pictures to illustrate those stories. He thoughtfully composed his images to show his subjects and the lives that created the expressions on their faces. Parks photographed moments in history.

Gordon Roger Alexander Buchanan Parks was born in Fort Scott, Kansas, in 1912. His father, Jackson, was a handyman and a farmer. His mother, Sarah, raised their 15 children. Parks was the youngest.

When Parks went to elementary school, it was a **segregated** experience. That meant white children went to the "whites-only" school. Black children went to the "Blacks-only" school. Parks was born into a nation where racism was rampant.

At 11 years old, three young white men threw Parks into the Marmaton River, determined to end his life. Parks held his breath underwater until he washed downstream.

He climbed out only when he was sure they could no longer see him.

Parks understood there were two Americas—one for white citizens, and one for Black citizens. But he wasn't willing to accept the limitations. He was bold enough to ask for success, and he eventually found it through the lens of a camera.

Working as a waiter for the Northern Pacific Railroad, Parks discovered powerful photographs of migrant workers in a discarded magazine. He was haunted by the pictures. He saved his money and bought his first camera at a **pawn shop**. By the time he was 25, Parks knew photography was his destiny.

Parks landed his first paying job as a photographer at a department store in St. Paul, Minnesota. Marva Louis, the wife of world-famous boxing champion Joe Louis, saw his work and suggested he move to Chicago, Illinois, to take portraits.

Parks met powerful Black artists, including painter Charles White and writer Langston Hughes, and took their portraits. He also documented poverty and racial injustice, like the injustice he had survived as a child. In 1941, his photographs of poor Black people in Chicago won him the Julius Rosenwald Fellowship—$200 dollars a month for a year to expand his art.

Next, Parks was hired by the Farm Security Administration (FSA) in Washington, DC. He was asked to photograph the plight of poor farmers, but as he walked

> **"ENTHUSIASM IS THE ELECTRICITY OF LIFE. HOW DO YOU GET IT? YOU ACT ENTHUSIASTIC UNTIL YOU MAKE IT A HABIT."**

into the FSA building in 1942, he noticed Ella Watson, an African American woman cleaning the floors. He took the time to talk with her, to understand who she was and how she felt.

As she stood holding a broom in one hand and a mop in the other, Parks remembered a classic painting called *American Gothic*. It features a man in overalls holding a pitchfork, standing beside his daughter. With that inspiration, Parks knew how to take Ella's portrait—with her holding her tools in front of a giant American flag. *Washington, D.C. Government Charwoman (American Gothic)* became one of his most famous photographs because Black workers had never been respectfully photographed before.

When the FSA closed, Parks moved to New York and got work as a freelance photographer for *Vogue*. The fashion magazine didn't usually hire Black photographers, but they let Parks shoot evening gowns after seeing his department store fashion photos. Instead of shooting the models standing still, Parks often shot them in motion, capturing the lovely flow of the fabric. He was the first to use this amazing photographic technique.

In New York, Parks met Red Jackson, the 17-year-old leader of the Midtowners, a Harlem gang. Parks earned his trust and spent weeks photographing gang life. He asked *Life Magazine*, America's most popular magazine, if they wanted to publish a photo essay on the Harlem gang, and they agreed. Parks captured the violence and the humanity of young men trapped in hopelessness.

Editors had hundreds of pictures to tell a well-balanced story. But they picked 21 images that reflected only violence and danger. Parks was disappointed, but he took a job as a staff photographer. On staff, he could control which pictures were used to tell more accurate stories.

In time, Parks became a filmmaker, directing *The Learning Tree* in 1969, based on his semi-autobiography, and *Shaft* in 1971. His movies inspired new Black filmmakers, including Spike Lee.

Parks built a legacy of photographic truth and talent. He captured powerful moments in history when he created portraits of African American heroes like Langston Hughes, Muhammad Ali, and Malcolm X. But he also immortalized ordinary people working hard to survive. He broke down racial barriers in his own life and opened doors for generations yet to come.

Gordon Parks was a revolutionary behind a camera lens. He was unyielding in his determination to expand the American experience to include Black stories of struggle and success. Those photographs are displayed in museum exhibits across the United States. They are celebrated for Parks's ability to speak volumes with a single image.

When he died in 2006, he was buried in Fort Scott, Kansas, next to his mother. His inspiration will live on for generations.

EXPLORE MORE! A museum dedicated to Gordon Parks is curated at the Fort Scott Community College in Kansas. You can see his photographs and personal effects through the virtual museum tour at GordonParksCenter.org.

DID YOU KNOW? In 1990, Gordon Parks, a student of music, created a ballet called *Martin* that honored the life of civil rights leader Reverend Martin Luther King Jr.

Andy
WARHOL
1928—1987

Andy Warhol is best known as a leading figure in the Pop Art movement—an energized combination of celebrities or objects **infused** with vibrant colors. One famous example is Warhol's 1962 Campbell's soup can series. In 32 nearly identical paintings—one representing each flavor Campbell's produced at the time—the artist proved even familiar things could be transformed into art.

Andy Warhol was born Andrew Warhola on August 6, 1928, in Pittsburgh, Pennsylvania, to first-generation Slovakian immigrants Andrej and Julia. He had two older brothers, Pavol (Paul) and John.

Warhol's family lived in a two-room apartment with an outhouse, a separate structure for a toilet with no plumbing. It was during the Great Depression, a time when millions of Americans were poor and out of work. The Warholas felt lucky to have a home, but they moved into a place with a toilet and plumbing when Warhol was two.

At eight, he got sick with a rare and sometimes deadly disease called Sydenham chorea. It caused his body to jerk and twist uncontrollably, especially when he felt anxious. Bedridden on and off for two years, Warhol read comic books and celebrity magazines. His mother—an artist in her own right—gave Warhol his first art lessons, drawing and tracing, to lift his spirits. She also bought him his first camera.

When Warhol recovered and attended Holmes Elementary School, he had trouble making friends. His teacher suggested taking art classes at the Carnegie Institute in Pittsburgh. He showed such promise, his father saved to send Warhol to the Carnegie Institute of Technology—now known as Carnegie Mellon University—where he continued his art studies.

After he earned a degree in design, Warhol moved to New York City to launch a career in commercial art. In 1949, he illustrated an article in *Glamour* magazine and went on to illustrate for Tiffany & Company, Columbia Records, and *Vogue* magazine. Making art to advertise popular American products influenced the masterpieces he went on to create later.

When Hollywood star Marilyn Monroe died in 1962, Warhol grieved. As a tribute, he created *Gold Marilyn Monroe* through a silkscreen process using a **stencil** of the image and glue on silk fabric. Once he rolled ink over the glue and the stencil, only the parts of the Monroe picture he wanted were transferred onto the fabric through the mesh of the silk fabric. It was the first of his

> ## "IN THE FUTURE, EVERYONE WILL BE WORLD-FAMOUS FOR 15 MINUTES."

many celebrity silkscreen masterpieces and one of his most popular works of Pop Art.

That same year, Warhol created his silkscreen *Green Coca-Cola Bottles*—a posterlike image of 112 identical green glass bottles standing side by side. Using seven rows of 16 bottles, Warhol celebrated the United States—a place where anyone could buy a soft drink, rich or poor. "A Coke is a Coke," he said, "and no amount of money can get you a better Coke..."

The influence of Warhol's early work creating product advertisement illustrations is clear in his 1964 silkscreen called *Brillo Boxes*. Warhol thought the packaging for the cleaning product was "friendly," even if the material inside was rough. He created a silkscreen, this time on plywood boxes instead of silk in his art studio called The Factory.

When President Richard Nixon reached out to Communist Chinese leader Mao Zedong in 1972, Warhol found a new focus for his silkscreen art. In 1973, he created hundreds of prints in different sizes titled *Mao*, with pink cheeks and blue eye shadow.

Some were huge—15 feet by 10 feet—to remind the world of Mao's use of **propaganda**. Mao tried to make himself look more important than he really was. The fact that Warhol made 199 nearly identical Mao paintings was his way of saying Mao was like a product sold in a grocery store.

For a time, Warhol was obsessed with death. But after a mentally ill writer shot Warhol in 1968 in his studio, the obsession faded. The bullets damaged his stomach, liver, spleen, and both lungs and forced him to wear a body brace for the rest of his life.

Thirteen years after the assault, in 1982, Warhol created *The Gun*. Using acrylic paint with his silkscreen technique on canvas, Warhol produced a huge, black, white, and red version of the handgun used in his attempted murder. It questioned how American culture celebrated weapons meant to cut life short.

Andy Warhol died on February 22, 1987. But his legacy lives on. His popular prints make up one-sixth of all contemporary art sold in the world today. Galleries all over the world exhibit his original artwork, and art fans still line up to experience them, decades after his death.

Warhol believed that every aspect of American life, from soup cans to soda bottles to popular celebrities, could be transformed into Pop Art. Some said his work was cold and revealed no emotion. But every color, every texture, every object is like a mirror and a criticism of

America's obsession with materialism, or owning lots of things.

Warhol proved that art could evolve and adapt to a changing world. He proved playfulness had a place on the world's museum walls, as well as on the walls of average art fans' homes.

EXPLORE MORE! Make your own Pop Art like Andy Warhol! Fold a sheet of paper into quarters and draw one iconic object four times. Color each object using different colors.

DID YOU KNOW? Andy Warhol collected taxidermy. He had the stuffed, preserved bodies of a lion, a peacock, a penguin, and a Great Dane he named Cecil.

Yayoi
KUSAMA
1929—

Yayoi Kusama is known worldwide for her contemporary paintings, sculptures, and infinity rooms. Her signature repeating design focuses on polka dots. For decades, she tried to launch her artistic vision, and for decades she was rejected. Against all odds, Kusama finally found global popularity and wealth, but she didn't care. Art remained her only focus.

Kusama was born on March 22, 1929, the youngest of four children, to a wealthy family in Matsumoto, Japan. Her parents ran a plant nursery and seed farm, so she found herself surrounded by flowers from an early age.

She was intrigued by drawing. Kusama carried a sketchbook everywhere, trying to capture the images that amazed her. Sadly, **schizophrenia** with **hallucinations** impacted her early life. Kusama imagined the flowers she drew spoke to her, and it frightened her.

The only thing that gave Kusama comfort was drawing, especially drawing polka dots. Her joy in her art enraged her mother, who was determined that Kusama would grow up to marry a wealthy man and be a wife only—never an artist. Insisting Kusama would never draw again, her mother destroyed all her art supplies to make her point.

Desperate to escape an unhappy life, Kusama wrote to Georgia O'Keeffe, a famous American painter who also loved flowers. O'Keeffe responded, saying it was hard to make a living as an artist in America, but if Kusama wanted to try, she should move to New York City.

Kusama knew very little English, and Japanese people were limited by how much money they could carry into the United States. So Kusama sewed money into the lining of her kimonos—dozens of lovely silk robes—and crossed the Pacific Ocean. If the money didn't last, Kusama planned to sell the kimonos to survive.

Some New York art critics loved Kusama's early work. But most museums refused to show a woman's creations. To make things worse, male artists in New York stole Kusama's ideas.

One art form that remained uniquely her own was Kusama's series of *Infinity Nets* paintings. To manage her visions of dots covering her hallucinations, she painted rows and rows of the patterns using red and black oil paint and canvases. Her art therapy became one of her first artistic success stories in 1959.

Kusama extended her *Infinity Nets* to sofas and armchairs in the 1960s. Instead of dots in oil paint, she covered the furniture in soft fabric-stuffed **appendages**. It was as if the dots had come to life and expanded before

> ## "MY LIFE IS A DOT LOST AMONG THOUSANDS OF OTHER DOTS."

her eyes. She called the series *Compulsion Furniture*. Some said they looked like fields of waving seaweed.

Kusama was not invited to show at the 1966 Venice Biennale, the Olympics of modern art in Italy. Instead, she independently set up her *Narcissus Garden* just outside the official location. As her audience explored 1,500 mirrored balls covering the ground, Kusama handed people individual orbs. People discovered they could see their own faces distorted by the round mirrors. Kusama sold the balls for a few dollars each. Italian art officials and police scolded her and shut her down for selling art like hot dogs. But in doing so, Kusama made art available to lower income admirers.

One of Kusama's most successful creations is her *Infinity Mirror Rooms*. Huge, mirrored rooms filled with lush carpeting and polka-dot creations appealed to art lovers and made Kusama's dream come true. Since her first childhood hallucinations in the flower gardens of Japan, Kusama wished she could climb into an unending world of polka dots. Her *Infinity Rooms* made it possible. And while she exhibited the first one in 1965, only to have it copied by another artist, they came to worldwide fame at Italy's 1993 Venice Biennale.

Today, thousands of art fans clamor to spend 30 seconds in one of Kusama's *Infinity Rooms* to take polka-dot–filled selfies. There are even detailed instructions online to help Kusama fans capture their best photo of a photo of a photo in the mirrors.

After an **emotional breakdown** in New York in 1977, Kusama went to live in a mental hospital in Tokyo, where she continues to live today. What could have been the end of her artistic career became her saving grace. Without the pressure of having to earn a living, she can work peacefully—sometimes for as long as 50 to 60 hours at a time.

Her visions became artistic sparks, and they allowed her to leave an enduring legacy for the contemporary and Pop Art world. Her drive to create art with repetition and patterns reminded the world of how busy life had become, and of how beautiful that chaos could be.

The Yayoi Kusama Museum opened in Tokyo in 2017, across the street from her hospital home. Kusama plans to create art until she takes her very last breath on Earth—art that is unforgettable.

EXPLORE MORE! Can you use polka dots to create art? Take a scrap of solid color cloth and tape it to cardboard. Now create your own work of art using polka dots of paint or marker ink.

DID YOU KNOW? On the TV series *Blown Away*, glassblower Momoko Schafer paid tribute to Kusama in a Pop Art challenge by making a polka-dot razor to honor her.

Jaune Quick-to-See
SMITH
1940—

Using a combination of paint and collage, Jaune Quick-to-See Smith creates abstract, multimedia art to illustrate her vision of life for **Indigenous Peoples** in the United States. Her work is not only beautiful and emotionally moving, but it also expresses an important Indigenous point of view that is too often overlooked.

Jaune Quick-to-See Smith was born on January 15, 1940, in St. Ignatius, Montana. As a member of the Confederated Salish and Kootenai Tribes, she grew up on the Flathead Reservation. Her mother left Smith and her sister when she was only two. Her father, a gifted horseman, cared for them and drew animals for Smith to keep. Those drawings led Smith to an artistic destiny.

Because money was tight, Smith traveled with her father from job to job. At the age of eight, she went to work to help her family survive but wound up in foster care. Forced to attend public elementary schools, she experienced the full force of racism that's all too often focused on Indigenous children.

As difficult as her childhood was, Smith pushed forward to finish her formal education. She earned her bachelor of arts in art education at Framingham State College in Massachusetts, and her master of arts at the University of New Mexico.

As she built her artistic career, Smith had two children and worked as a librarian, a janitor, a veterinary assistant, and a factory worker. Day after day, she fought for her rightful place in the American world of fine art. It was a fight she eventually won.

Inspired by the work of Pablo Picasso and the artwork of her ancestry, Smith hoped to preserve and elevate her heritage and speak for her people's history, environmental concerns, and political demands.

Using newspaper clippings, photographs, and textbook pages, Smith creates painted collages that express her important point of view. She feels white Americans see the land as property to own, but Indigenous Peoples see it as a living entity. The wind, the wildlife, and the weather all create life in Smith's culture. That mindset has been a part of Smith's art for her entire career.

In 1992, Smith created *I See Red: Target*, an 11-foot-tall work now on permanent exhibit at the National Gallery of Art (NGA) in Washington, DC. It was the first work created by an Indigenous person ever purchased by the NGA, and it is on exhibit next to art by Andy Warhol. Smith created it in response to the 500th anniversary of Christopher Columbus's mistreatment of Indigenous Peoples.

> **"I SEE MYSELF AS A BRIDGE BUILDER . . . I GO FROM ONE COMMUNITY WITH MESSAGES TO THE OTHER, AND I TRY TO ENLIGHTEN PEOPLE."**

In two canvases, Smith creates a painful reflection of abuse, using a dartboard at the top of the work, the headline "Destroy the Myth" just below it, and a half circle of feather-like darts on top of the board. The rest of the large collage features examples of Indigenous **appropriation** and racial **slurs**, like sports banners, along with clippings from mainstream newspapers and the *Char-Koosta News*, the Flathead Reservation paper. Dripping with bloodred paint, it reminds the art world of the mistreatment of Smith's ancestors.

The same year, Smith created *Trade (Gifts for Trading Land with White People)*. Another collage of news clippings and oil paint, the crimson outline of a canoe is spread across the whole work and a string of worthless trinkets dangle above the canvas on a metal chain.

Trade pushes back against the colonial idea that Indigenous Peoples were naive enough to make such a meaningless trade as taking $24 from the Dutch settlers for the island of Manhattan. The story is not true and sets a disrespectful tone in describing Indigenous Peoples. Smith's work demands a reexamination of these events.

State Names, created in 2000, is a large map of the United States. Drips and brushstrokes of turquoise, gold, white, and rust-colored oil paint cover state names not inspired by the Indigenous Peoples who once populated the land. Now on exhibit at the Smithsonian American Art Museum, it highlights state names like Wyoming, a Delaware Indian word that means "mountains and valleys alternating," and Kansas, a Lakota word meaning "people of the south wind."

Jaune Quick-to-See Smith's legacy has many branches. Her personal history as an Indigenous person serves to encourage other Indigenous artists in need of a role model. Her work also offers a legacy of awareness. She remembers the abuse heaped on Indigenous Peoples. She has also spent a lifetime trying to artistically document the nightmares and seek lasting justice. This includes protesting against ancestral lands having been forcibly taken from Indigenous Peoples, with no respect for their tribal territories or distant history in the regions.

Smith has passed her papers and sketches on to the Joan Mitchell Foundation—an artistic storage library that protects the past for generations to come. She has taught others how to express their own artistic ideals, even as they turn to her work for inspiration. And she has sold her work to museums and collectors all over the world, to be sure additional eyes are opened to Indigenous truths so often ignored.

Smith's legacy is not just her art; it is her life. And it has been a life very well spent.

EXPLORE MORE! You can see Smith's *State Names* and a second unnamed work featuring four bison in a colorful collage at the Smithsonian American Art Museum in Washington, DC.

DID YOU KNOW? Smith has called her work "Nomad Art." With respect for the Indigenous ideal of "take only what you need from the Earth," many of her collages use biodegradable materials.

Jean-Michel
BASQUIAT
1960–1988

Jean-Michel Basquiat started as a New York City **graffiti** artist in the late 1970s. Within three years, his street art evolved into a Neo-Expressionist style that made him famous. His bold, recognizable work celebrated bright colors, serious topics, and the importance of African American life. He was young and creative and willing to work hard to prove his talent was real.

Jean-Michel Basquiat was born in Brooklyn, New York, on December 22, 1960, the second of four children. His mother was Puerto Rican, and his father was from Haiti, so Basquiat grew up fluent in English, Spanish, and French.

Basquiat showed a talent for art early in his life, drawing on paper his father brought home from work. His mother often took him to New York's many art museums. By the time he was six, Basquiat was a junior member of the Brooklyn Museum.

At age eight, he was hit by a car while playing with friends in the street. His spleen was removed due to the accident. While recovering, Basquiat was given a copy of *Gray's Anatomy*, an important medical book about the human body. This book made a strong impression on him and his future art.

Basquiat also read comic books and watched cartoons. His interests helped him create street art that would launch his career. Basquiat found life increasingly difficult at home. He quit high school in 1977 to pursue art full-time. Often homeless, he pushed on. He signed his street art with a three-pointed crown, which became a well-recognized symbol for him. The crown was Basquiat's way of reminding the world that Black people were important.

After struggling for three years, Basquiat found fame in June 1980, when his work moved from being created on trains and brick walls to discarded objects and later canvases displayed at the Times Square Show. Street art could only be seen on the street. But art that could be moved, admired, and sold changed the young artist's life. Two years later, he had his own exhibition at a SoHo gallery. Now called a Neo-Expressionist—a modern artist willing to create recognizable figures—he no longer had to worry about paying his bills.

La Hara, a fiery reflection of Basquiat's frustration with police brutality, was painted in 1981. It features a policeman behind bars, his blue hat against a bright red background, and his eyes blazing red. "La Hara" is Puerto Rican slang for a police officer.

> # "I DON'T THINK ABOUT ART WHEN I WORK . . . I TRY TO THINK ABOUT LIFE."

Basquiat painted *Warrior* in 1982. The focus of the artwork is a skeletal figure wearing a green crown and swinging a massive, white sword. Its eyes seem angry, and its two feet seem oversized compared to the rest of the figure's body. Bright blocks of yellow and blue surround the warrior, standing in a sea of lighter yellow. A halo surrounds the warrior's head, and it is thought to be a self-portrait.

Flesh and Spirit, a huge painting Basquiat created from 1982 to 1983, was one of his rare works in neutral colors. It contains black-and-white blocks covered with skeletal and fleshy features of the human body. Descriptions—of brains, ribs, femurs, throats—are scribbled in words beside them. The title was inspired by a book called *Flash of the Spirit* that celebrated the beauty of African art. Basquiat may have been celebrating African art, too.

Between 1984 and 1985, Basquiat joined forces with one of his artistic idols, Andy Warhol. Warhol began a work with an iconic silkscreen image, like he did in *Zenith* in 1984, and Basquiat added his free-flowing strokes to the creation. People said Warhol was using the young painter to get attention. But the close friendship produced almost 200 paintings.

In the Wings, painted in 1986, was Basquiat's tribute to jazz saxophonist Lester Young. The Black musician, dressed in a green suit and hat, holds his golden sax in a sea of rich blue. A sign above his head reads "Reno Club." Basquiat painted a lot of important Black musicians, including Young, Charlie Parker, Dizzy Gillespie, Duke Ellington, and Billie Holiday. Elevating Black excellence was very important to him.

In 1988, Basquiat died at the age of 27. In his short life of 27 years, Basquiat created more than 600 paintings and 1,500 drawings.

Basquiat never studied art. He studied the world. His legacy was his ability to absorb all the things he saw and experienced and turn those things into art. He was inspired by other creators, but his creations were his own.

His legacy is also his hunger. Basquiat was driven to make art and to achieve the fame that would prove his art was good. As a teenager, he boldly chased Andy Warhol into a restaurant and asked him to buy his art postcards. Warhol bought one or two.

Once Basquiat claimed his fame, he fought to remain true to himself, wearing paint-splattered suits and posing barefoot for magazine covers. Basquiat was a true original. His life was cut short, but his art lives on. And if his art exists, so does his spirit.

EXPLORE MORE! Basquiat used a combination of drawings and powerful words to create some of his artwork. Draw your favorite thing, then add words to describe how that object makes you feel. See if Basquiat's secrets can open up artistic magic in you.

DID YOU KNOW? Basquiat sold his first painting for $200 to punk rocker Debbie Harry of the band Blondie. He also appeared as a DJ in her video for the song "Rapture."

Njideka
AKUNYILI CROSBY
1983—

Njideka Akunyili Crosby is an observer. She studies important matters—love, family, racism—and uses mixed media techniques to capture the feelings they inspire in art. Akunyili Crosby marries painting, photography, and fabric to create emotionally powerful, giant collages. She calls her work a hybrid—the joining of elements to create new beauty.

In 1983, Akunyili Crosby was born in Enugu, Nigeria. One of six children, her parents were educated professionals. Her father, J.C. Akunyili, was a surgeon and a university professor. Her mother, Dora, was a professor of pharmacology—the study of how drugs interact with the human body—and a public servant in government.

At 10, Akunyili Crosby's family moved from a small town in southeastern Nigeria to the bustling city life of Lagos. Accepted to a top-notch girls' boarding school away from home, Akunyili Crosby's world transformed as she found herself surrounded by people from all walks of life, including "bobblers," wealthy girls who traveled broadly and watched American television shows like *Friends*.

At 16, she and her sister Ijeoma were granted the right to study in the United States. Akunyili Crosby studied independently for a year to pass her **SAT tests** to qualify for classes at the Community College of Philadelphia. She took her first painting class there and discovered her artistic destiny.

A teacher told Akunyili Crosby to apply to Swarthmore College, and she was accepted in 2004. She studied art and biology, then she continued her studies at the Pennsylvania Academy of the Fine Arts. She was awarded her master of fine arts degree from Yale School of Art.

Home for Njideka Akunyili Crosby is in two places. She has citizenship in both the United States and Nigeria. Like her groundbreaking art, she also is a hybrid, a combination of both worlds.

Akunyili Crosby spends hours planning her projects. Parts are painted. Parts are photographic transfers—repeating photographs cut into shapes. Parts are Nigerian fabric patterns. Every inch reflects who she is or who she has been.

I Refuse to be Invisible was created in 2010. It is roughly 10 feet tall and 7 feet wide and crafted in ink, charcoal, acrylic paint, and photographic transfers. It features a young couple standing on a crowded dance floor. The man's face and arms are made of a collage of photo transfers, as is the woman's dress. But the woman's face

> **"YOU DON'T EXIST IF YOU'RE NOT REPRESENTED. I FELT A NEED TO CLAIM MY OWN SOCIAL EXISTENCE BY MAKING THE REPRESENTATION HAPPEN."**

is painted in warm, brown acrylic tones, and she gazes at you—the stranger exploring the art.

The clothes are global in fashion styles, but the patterns on the clothes reflect Nigerian traditions. Akunyili Crosby reveals the painting is autobiographical about her romance with her husband. But it is very much a hybrid of lifestyles and materials.

In *Wedding Portrait*, created in 2012, Akunyili Crosby offers a glimpse of her wedding in Nigeria, using a canvas a little over 5 feet wide and 4 ½ feet tall. She is seen kneeling at her husband's feet as she offers him a cup of palm wine. Once he takes the cup and tastes the wine, they are married.

Her groom's white face is blocked by other people attending the wedding. But his arm can be seen as he takes the cup from his African bride. Her shoulders, face, and arms are painted without transfers in rich, beautiful brown tones. Akunyili Crosby is telling us her past and her future have come together to create a beautiful new beginning—a blending of cultures, brought together through love.

Mother and Child, composed in 2016 when Akunyili Crosby was expecting her first child, was created with acrylic paint, photographic transfers, colored pencils, and commemorative fabric. In Nigeria, special occasions are marked by the creation of "portrait fabrics," patterned cloth with repeated portraits of the person being celebrated.

A beautiful African woman in an elegant, patterned dress sits in a yellow chair, looking past the black-and-white portrait of a mother and a child hanging on the wall. The portrait is of Akunyili Crosby's grandmother holding her youngest aunt. The wallpaper is portrait cloth created when the artist's mother ran for office in Nigeria.

Njideka Akunyili Crosby is a relatively new artist. Her legacy is still unfolding, but it is a celebration of diversity and differences. Her art reflects both of her homes, and both of her cultural traditions. It represents her life as a gifted Black woman from Nigeria, married to a white American man. Her legacy is the beauty of blending things that are different but equally worthwhile.

In each of Akunyili Crosby's pieces, we witness a very personal glimpse into her hybrid life. She celebrates her own African heritage and ancestry. She also embraces her white American husband and biracial child with just as much passion.

She uses her personal life and her textured art to remind the world that peaceful unity is possible. Neither side of the equation is better than the other. But together, they create something special for all the world to see.

EXPLORE MORE! Mixing media is central to Akunyili Crosby's style. Create your own mixed media art piece by making a collage of meaningful photos, scraps of cloth, and paint.

DID YOU KNOW? Akunyili Crosby sometimes uses marble dust in her artwork. It's actually calcium carbonate dust, and it adds grit and texture to paint.

Glossary

appendages: small things attached to something larger and more important, like fingers on a hand or toes on a foot.

apprenticed: learning a trade from an experienced tradesperson, usually at a young age.

appropriation: using one culture's symbols in another culture without permission or respect.

asylum: a place where mentally disabled people can seek help from doctors and protection from people who fear or dislike them.

Buddhist: a spiritual practice inspired by a teacher named Gautama Buddha from India.

Charles Darwin: a naturalist who collected evidence to prove evolution was real and lived in 19th century England.

cholera epidemic: an infection caused by eating food with a bacteria called *Vibrio cholerae*. An epidemic is a huge number of infections.

diphtheria: a contagious disease that makes it hard to breathe and can damage the heart.

eccentric: brave enough to act differently than most people act. It's a kinder way to say someone is weird.

emotional breakdown: also known as a nervous breakdown, it occurs when a person is no longer able to function normally; often indicates a mental health problem that needs attention.

frail: weak and fragile because of old age or illness.

graffiti: writing and drawing applied to walls with paint, sometimes without permission. Street art is a more formal kind of graffiti.

hallucinations: seeing things that are not there due to mental illness or drug use.

Harlem Renaissance: a period spanning from 1918 to 1937 that celebrated African American art, music, dance, literature, theater, and politics in New York City's Harlem neighborhood.

immersive: when a piece of art surrounds or involves the person viewing it.

Indigenous Peoples: a people who are the earliest inhabitants of a specific region.

infused: filled with. When you open a curtain, the room is infused with light. When you make lemonade, water is infused with lemon juice.

medallions: flattened circles or ovals used for decorating rooms or creating jewelry and awards.

muted: softened, as in the quieting of a sound or the lightening of a color.

naturalist: a scientist who studies animals in the natural world, not in cages or zoos.

pawn shop: a store where people can sell valuable items for money.

polio: an infectious disease of the nervous system that can cause paralysis—the inability to walk or move.

portraits: artwork that features only a person's or animal's face, not their whole body.

propaganda: the spreading of information or rumors to help or harm a person.

risqué: shocking or embarrassing behavior, like running through the street without clothing.

samurai: ancient Japanese male warrior who had power in his country.

SAT tests: tests designed to measure a high school student's knowledge after all their classes have been completed.

schizophrenia: a mental illness that blurs the line between what is real and what is not real.

segregated: divided into groups based on skin color, wealth, or gender.

seminary: a school that prepares an adult person to be a religious leader.

slurs: insults that are often based on race, disabilities, genders, or body types.

stencil: a plastic or cardboard sheet with cutout designs to be reproduced using paint or other art supplies.

symbolism: the use of objects to represent ideas. The American flag is a symbol of the country. The dove is a symbol of peace.

terra-cotta: objects made using a red clay, also called terra-cotta.

Victorian-era: the time period between 1820 and 1914 that overlapped with Queen Victoria's reign of the United Kingdom from 1837 to 1901.

widow: a woman left alone by the death of her husband. Men left alone by the death of their wives are called widowers.

References

Baillie, Rebecca. "Julia Margaret Cameron." The Art Story. August 7, 2018. TheArtStory.org/artist /cameron-julia-margaret/artworks/.

BBC. "History: Michelangelo (1475–1564)." BBC. 2014. BBC.co.uk/history/historic_figures /michelangelo.shtml.

Biography.com Editors. "Pablo Picasso Biography." Biography.com. Last updated August 28, 2019. Biography.com/artist/pablo-picasso.

Biography. "Michelangelo: Artist & Genius | Full Documentary | BIOGRAPHY." YouTube. July 2, 2021. YouTube.com/watch?v=GnK9pwjg-9A.

Brown, Emily. "Andy Warhol and His Artistic Influence." Culture Trip. September 6, 2016. TheCultureTrip.com /north-america/usa/new-york/new-york-city /articles/andy-warhol-and-his-artistic-influence.

Burke, Alden. "Gordon Parks: Biography and Legacy." The Art Story. August 25, 2018. TheArtStory.org /artist/parks-gordon/life-and-legacy.

Church, Lewis. "Jean-Michel Basquiat: Biography and Legacy." The Art Story. November 22, 2011. TheArtStory .org/artist/basquiat-jean-michel/life-and-legacy.

Cotter, Holland. "Bernini, the Man of Many Heads."
New York Times. August 7, 2008. NYTimes.com
/2008/08/08/arts/design/08bern.html.

Gotthardt, Alexxa. "6 Works That Explain Yayoi Kusama's
Rise to Art World Stardom." Artsy. June 21, 2018.
Artsy.net/article/artsy-editorial-6-works-explain
-yayoi-kusamas-rise-art-stardom.

Greenberger, Alex. "Before Yayoi Kusama Made 'Infinity
Rooms,' She Created Standout Political Works."
ARTnews. May 18, 2020. ArtNews.com/feature
/yayoi-kusama-most-famous-works-1202687572.

Greenberger, Alex. "5 Works to Know by Bernini: Ornate
Canopies, Billowing Fabrics, and More." *ARTnews.*
July 30, 2021. ArtNews.com/list/art-news/artists/gian
-lorenzo-bernini-most-famous-works-1234600353
/apollo-and-daphne-sciopioni-borghese.

Ingram, Sarah. "Utagawa Hiroshige: Biography and
Legacy." The Art Story. April 9, 2019. TheArtStory.org
/artist/hiroshige-utagawa/life-and-legacy.

Jones, Jonathan. "And the Winner Is . . ." *Guardian.*
October 22, 2002. TheGuardian.com/culture/2002
/oct/22/artsfeatures.highereducation.

León, Concepción de. "The Black Woman Artist Who Crafted a Life She Was Told She Couldn't Have." *New York Times*. March 30, 2021. NYTimes.com/2021 /03/30/us/augusta-savage-black-woman-artist -harlem-renaissance.html.

Lewis, Mary Tompkins. "'Berthe Morisot, Woman Impressionist' Review: A Legacy Restored." *Wall Street Journal*. March 19, 2019. WSJ.com/articles/berthe -morisot-woman-impressionist-review-a-legacy -restored-11553021609.

Mafi, Nick. "A Painting by Pablo Picasso Is Now Collectively Owned by 25,000 Strangers." *Architectural Digest*. May 1, 2018. ArchitecturalDigest.com/story /painting-pablo-picasso-collectively-owned -25000-strangers.

New Mexico State University. Saul Ramirez, researcher. "Jaune Quick-to-See Smith: The Work and the Artist." University Art Museum. November 24, 2016. UAM.nmsu.edu/jaune-quick-to-see-smith.

PBS. "How Self-Taught Photographer Gordon Parks Became a Master Storyteller." *PBS News Hour*. YouTube. February 1, 2019. YouTube.com/watch?v =gQLUbdp7fqA.

Pitz, Marylynne. "Andy Warhol's Childhood." The Digs: From the Photo Archives of the *Pittsburgh Post-Gazette*. May 19, 2014. NewsInteractive.post-gazette.com/thedigs/2014/05/19/andy-warhols-childhood.

Pound, Cath. "Yayoi Kusama's Extraordinary Survival Story." BBC. September 26, 2018. BBC.com/culture/article/20180925-yayoi-kusamas-extraordinary-survival-story.

Schjeldahl, Peter. "Berthe Morisot, 'Woman Impressionist,' Emerges from the Margins." *New Yorker*. October 22, 2018. NewYorker.com/magazine/2018/10/29/berthe-morisot-woman-impressionist-emerges-from-the-margins.

Selvin, Claire. "What's the Best Painting by Van Gogh? Eight Experts Reveal Their Favorite Works." *ARTnews*. April 21, 2020. ArtNews.com/art-news/artists/vincent-van-gogh-best-paintings-1202684383.

Smithsonian. "Augusta Savage." Smithsonian American Art Museum. Accessed August 2021. AmericanArt.si.edu/artist/augusta-savage-4269.

Solway, Diane. "Nigerian Artist Njideka Akunyili Crosby Is Painting the Afropolitan Story in America." *W Magazine*. August 15, 2017. WMagazine.com/story/njideka-akunyili-crosby-artist-painter.

Stamberg, Susan. "Sculptor Augusta Savage Said Her Legacy Was the Work of Her Students." NPR. July 15, 2019. NPR.org/2019/07/15/740459875/sculptor -augusta-savage-said-her-legacy-was-the-work-of -her-students.

Vankin, Deborah. "Njideka Akunyili Crosby: The Painter in Her MacArthur Moment." *Los Angeles Times*. November 2, 2017. LATimes.com/entertainment/arts /la-ca-cm-njideka-akunyili-crosby-20171102 -htmlstory.html.

White, Simone. "Skin, or Surface: Njideka Akunyili Crosby." *Frieze*, March 9, 2018. Frieze.com/article /skin-or-surface-njideka-akunyili-crosby.

Wulfhorst, Ellen. "Pablo Picasso: The Life Story You May Not Know." *Stacker*. May 19, 2021. Stacker.com /stories/12763/pablo-picasso-life-story-you -may-not-know.

About the Author

 **Kelly Milner Halls** loved drawing when she was a kid. She knew she wasn't good enough to be a professional artist, but she was good enough to recognize fine art. Instead of making art for a living, she decided to write true stories—nonfiction—for kids. She's published more than 50 books, but she knows the best books include wonderful art. She is grateful to the artists who've helped make her books worthwhile. For more about Kelly and her work, visit WondersofWeird.com.

About the Illustrator

 **Amy Blackwell** is an artist and a creative dabbler. She paints, prints, knits, scribbles, or does whatever takes her creative fancy at the time. She is based in the midlands—Nottingham to be exact—and has a small studio space in town where the magic happens. Amy is inspired by the weird and wonderful, clashing colors, the natural world, history, fashion, and folklore. Usually if there's an opportunity to draw patterns on something, she will give it her best shot.